MW01657101

감사합니다!

Thank you for purchasing this Hangeul workbook!

This book is designed to be used with audio recordings. To download these along with FREE enrollment into our interactive Hangeul course, please email us your purchase code to admin@teachmekorean.co

To continue your Korean studies with one-on-one tutored help and fun interactive courses, please join us over at:

http://teachmekorean.co.uk/

Published 2017

Chapters

01 Hangeul Basics

Without referring to the Hangeul Bootcamp book, answer the following questions based on your knowledge of Hangeul.

1. Around which year was Hangeul created?

2. After the creation, elite literates gave Hangeul which nickname?

3. The individual letters are known as what?

4. How many Hangeul characters are there in total?

5. There are a total of how many consonants in Korean?

6. How many 'Diphthong' vowels are there in Korean?

02 Simple Vowels

Practice writing the Hangeul letters in the correct stroke order.

ㅏ

ㅓ

ㅗ

ㅜ

ㅡ

ㅣ

ㅐ

ㅔ

03 Basic Consonants

ㄱ

ㄴ

ㄷ

ㄹ

ㅁ

ㅂ

ㅅ

ㅇ

ㅈ

Pronunciation Practice

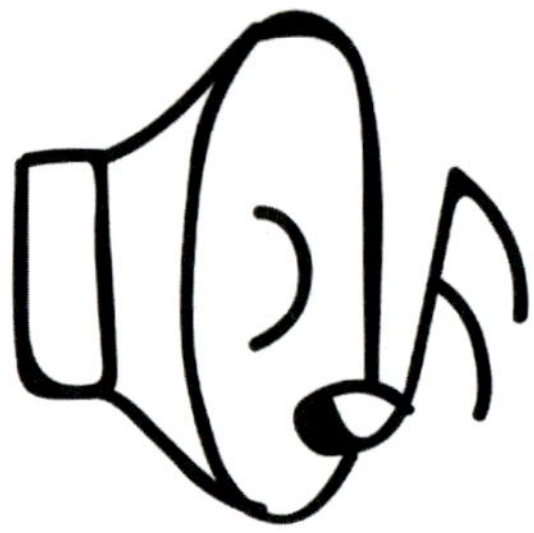

1. Listen to "track 1" and write the vowels being pronounced.

1	2	3	4	5	6

2. Listen to "track 2" and circle the words you hear.

1. 간 단 강
2. 데 대 레
3. 즈 주 스
4. 노무 너므 너무
5. 고기 거기 저기
6. 나이 다이 니아

3. Listen to "track 3" and simply write the words you hear.

1. ____________
2. ____________
3. ____________
4. ____________
5. ____________
6. ____________
7. ____________

04 Iotized Vowels

ㅑ					
ㅕ					
ㅛ					
ㅠ					
ㅒ					
ㅖ					

1. Listen to "track 4" and write the vowels being pronounced.

1	2	3	4	5	6

05 Aspirated Consonants

ㅋ					
ㅌ					
ㅍ					
ㅊ					
ㅎ					

1. Listen to "track 5" and complete the missing syllables.

1. ____나다
2. 고____
3. 파____
4. 햄____거
5. ____지
6. 태____

Pronunciation Practice

1. Listen to "track 6" and complete the syllables with the missing consonants you can hear.

1	2	3	4	5	6
ㅑ	ㅗ	ㅕ	ㅠ	ㅣ	ㅖ

2. Listen to "track 7" and circle the words you hear being pronounced.

1. 사 자 차
2. 불 풀 물
3. 셔 서 죠
4. 갸 캬 탸
5. 후 우 휴
6. 공 콩 컹
7. 발 팔 퍌
8. 태 테 톄
9. 호 효 혀

06 Writing Practice # 1

Practice writing the vocabulary using the correct stroke order.

다시 Again	가수 Singer	노래 Song	식사 Meal

오늘 Today	겨울 Winter	배우 Actor / Actress	지혜 Wisdom

Writing Practice

연휴 Holiday	요리 Cooking	야채 Vegetables	프로 Professional

너무 Too, Very	토지 Land	크기 Size	마다 Every, Each

07 Diphthongs

ㅘ					
ㅙ					
ㅚ					
ㅝ					
ㅞ					
ㅟ					
ㅢ					

1. Listen to "track 8" and write the vowels being pronounced.

1	2	3	4	5	6

08 Double Consonants

ㄲ

ㄸ

ㅉ

ㅃ

ㅆ

1. Listen to "track 9" and complete the missing syllables.

1. ____자
2. 오____
3. ____다
4. 영____
5. ____자
6. 가____

Pronunciation Practice

1. Listen to "track 10" and circle the words you hear being pronounced.

1. 가 카 까
2. 휘 화 홰
3. 디 티 띠
4. 뷔 봐 퐈
5. 추 주 쭈
6. 와 위 의
7. 소 조 쏘
8. 브 프 쁘

2. Listen to "track 11" and write out the words you hear.

1. ____________	5. ____________	9. ____________
2. ____________	6. ____________	10. ____________
3. ____________	7. ____________	11. ____________
4. ____________	8. ____________	12. ____________

09 Writing Practice # 2

Write the following Konglish words in the correct stroke order.

카메라 Camera	피아노 Piano	바나나 Banana

햄버거 Hamburger	초콜릿 Chocolate	샤워 Shower

택시 Taxi	버스 Bus	아이스크림 Ice cream

Writing Practice

호텔 Hotel	메뉴 Menu	쇼핑 Shopping

섹시 Sexy	키스 Kiss	핸드폰 Cell Phone

팬티 Underwear	매니큐어 Nail Polish	미팅 Meeting

Writing Practice

사이다 Soda	사인 Autograph	스킨십 'Couple Touching'

탤런트 Actor / Actress	와이셔츠 Shirt	오픈 카 Convertible Car

오토바이 Motorcycle	글래머 'Big Breasted Woman'	아르바이트 Part Time Job

10 Borrowed English

1. Translate the following words into the English equivalent.

1 텔레비전 ______________________

2 달러 ______________________

3 주스 ______________________

4 테이블 ______________________

5 로맨스 ______________________

6 샴푸 ______________________

7 비디오 ______________________

8 쿠키 ______________________

9 게임 ______________________

10 스타벅스 ______________________

11 퀴즈 ______________________

12 오렌지 ______________________

13 크리스마스 ______________________

14 샌드위치 ______________________

2. Listen to "track 12" and write out the Konglish words you hear being pronounced. You should then translate them to what you think their English meaning is.

1 핫도그 Hot Dog

2

3

4

5

6

7

8

9

10

11

12

11 Pronunciation Rules

Read the word given, and using your knowledge of the Hangeul rules, choose from the following options the correct way to pronounce it.

1. 먹는다 — 먼는다 멉는다 멍는다
2. 받는다 — 반는다 방는다 밧는다
3. 신문로 — 신문오 신문료 신문노
4. 붙여요 — 부텨요 부쳐요 부저요
5. 백화점 — 배과점 배콰점 배하점
6. 신고 — 신노 신코 신꼬
7. 강가 — 강까 간까 간카
8. 맞히 — 마찌 마히 마치

12 Dictionary Order

1. Rank the following words in 'dictionary order'.

그럼	곳	옆	댁
	1		

싸다	고향	정말	취미

왠지	방	아빠	어깨
		8	

애교	팔	후회	며칠
	15		

2. Translate the following words using a Korean-English dictionary.

1 진짜 ________________

2 많이 ________________

3 큰 ________________

4 사진 ________________

5 여기 ________________

6 이름 ________________

7 학생 ________________

8 조금 ________________

9 음식 ________________

10 생일 ________________

11 간식 ________________

12 운동 ________________

13 책 ________________

14 집 ________________

15 너무 ________________

Congratulations!

You have completed the Hangeul Bootcamp course and can now read, write and pronounce Hangeul like a pro!

To check if the answers you gave in this workbook are correct, please visit the following link to use the interactive answer key:
http://teachmekorean.co.uk/answer-key/

If you have any questions, feel free to send us an email over at admin@teachmekorean.co

67529640R00015

Made in the USA
Lexington, KY
14 September 2017